Kathleen

Kathleen

A Record of a Sorrow

By E. M. Blaiklock

HODDER AND STOUGHTON
LONDON SYDNEY AUCKLAND TORONTO

British Library Cataloguing in Publication Data
Blaiklock, Edward Musgrave
   Kathleen.
1. Bereavement
  I. Title
248'.86   BV4905.2

ISBN 0 340 25158 1

Set, printed and bound in Great Britain for Hodder and
Stoughton Ltd., Mill Road, Dunton Green, Sevenoaks, Kent
by Cox & Wyman Ltd., Reading

And the earth was without form and void, and darkness was upon the face of the deep. And God said: 'Let there be light, and there was light.'

Foreword

IT was nearly twenty years since I first met Professor E. M. Blaiklock, and ten years since I started publishing for him, but it was only last summer that I was privileged to visit his home in Titirangi, Auckland, New Zealand. Six months earlier his wife, Kathleen, had died. I understood his agony, for a few years before I had lost my own dear partner.

Suddenly, I saw him no longer as the distinguished

former Professor of Classics in the University of Auckland, and the author of numerous books in the spheres of New Testament studies and Greek classical drama. I found myself loving as well as admiring him. He now belonged to the fellowship of those who know the most intense of personal bereavements.

I first knew of Kathleen's illness the previous August. 'Did you say that you are marrying again?' he wrote. 'Perhaps this is when I should wish you a blessed tract of fruitful living. I myself am sitting lonely in my library tonight having just taken my wife for tests in the Public Hospital. While we were abroad it became apparent that a growing dysphasia was the mark of a slight stroke.'

A month later he spoke of his wife's dire illness, and in October confided: 'The one who has talked to me, advised and admonished for forty-nine years of married life lives with undamaged intelligence so far, behind a wall of frustrating silence. We cannot even pray together, though she understands my words. The skies may grow darker yet. I have cancelled all engagements but find I can still write, and like our good friend C. S. Lewis,* I find some relief in doing so.'

Writing gave him strange relief, as his wife continued her stumbling path downwards. 'Her intelligence is intact, but I do everything for her with one

* See *A Grief Observed*.

arm gone and almost one leg,' he wrote in November. 'But, after all, forty-nine years ago I promised something about "in sickness and in health", and I am expendable when it comes to that.' In January, Kathleen was in hospital speechless, only partly responsive to his presence, paralysed. Her ordeal ended on February 8, 1978, when the deadly tumour finished its work and she passed peacefully.

The Professor wrote: 'My family are wonderful, but after years of the most wonderful close companionship, I live in what so far seems unbroken anguish. The house in these lonely hills is crowded with memories – every drawer, every cupboard ... But I must stop. I often find myself typing on for the sake of someone to talk to, and you, I think, having trudged this valley, seem to be one who will listen.'

I promised prayer. 'I desperately need it,' he replied. 'This contest with the last Enemy (and the ever-present Enemy of the Soul) goes on unabated.'

Sitting in his gracious but empty home in August I forgot that he had been the public orator of the University of Auckland, and a lecturer of international repute, who travelled widely in the study of biblical and classical archaeology. He was a lonely man struggling to cope with bereavement and with the same melancholy that I had known. I asked, hoping work would be an anodyne, whether he would prepare a new translation from the Latin of *The Imitation of Christ*, with a fresh introduction, and we also finalised arrangements for the *Blaiklock Bible Handbook*. The translation arrived in a few months but he had found little relief of heart and began to keep a diary.

Kathleen – a Record of a Sorrow is based on that diary. When he first shared the pages with me I knew it was almost too personal to publish, and to do so may be my indulgence, but my request was based on a belief that it may meet some needs more than most 'books of comfort' do.

EDWARD ENGLAND

Religious Publishing Director
Hodder & Stoughton
Summer 1979

Kathleen

February 4, 1979

SOME impulse bids me begin. 'Write about it,'
said the Dean of Auckland. 'Preach about it,'
said the Emeritus Dean of Saint Paul's and told me
of himself ... Perhaps John Rymer and Martin
Sullivan were right, and I should do so. I shall try.

February 8, the day she died as gently as she had
lived, is only just down the week, and I dread that
anniversary. This year has held eternity.

But begin this afternoon? I know why. All the tall

trees outside my library window are roaring aloud in an unaccustomed wind, the young kauris, a century old, a kawaka and a pohutukawa, which we two planted when we came to live on the hillside by the forest, thirty-three years ago . . .

They roared like this all the long summer evening the day she went away, stumbling along the path to the car, supported by the two loved women who had married her sons. Her speech was gone, her right leg no longer held her. That was November 29, 1977. She had ten more weeks before the Thing, the film creeping across the surface of her fine brain, finished its dire destruction. On my brain that scene is stamped forever, silver hair, brown check overcoat, right foot lifted on Marjorie's left. . .

I followed them the seven miles to David's home. He is a doctor, who owed his mother much in love and counsel. In the evening I came home to the desolate house. Just a house now, no longer the home her presence made it. I walked from room to room. Silent. But the Ents of the woodland would have no silence. They roared in grief, arms flailing, for the one who had loved them, and the void she had left for me and for them. That is four hundred and twenty-three days ago and they are talking again, protesting, striving, this Sunday afternoon as I sit at my desk remembering.

I am picturing again with equal clarity the day

she walked into my life to sanctify almost half a hundred years. It was November 13, 1928, white dress, white veil, on her grand old father's arm. I looked round to see, which they told me I should not have done, but how glad I am that I hold for ever that lovely picture. Thus she entered, and thus she went. My two Novembers . . .

A year has gone. Yes, 1978, and it has taught me only that memory holds the door wide open, with each day some agonising recall of sweetness and now vanished fellowship, some sombre recollection of pain. Yes, early February 1977: 'I think I have had a slight stroke,' she said, sitting before the great window with its vast view of the most beautifully sited city I know. 'I am confusing words.' We went abroad, hoping for gradual improvement, but the contrary was the case. Came August and optimistic diagnosis was abandoned. I said to the neurologist what he left me to say: 'Then I must watch her slowly die?' He did not reply, but kindly eyes said all there was to say.

That is what I did. I watched for six months. A year ago this week. The white room on Wednesday. The crowded cathedral on Friday. The words which her son, David, and Alison her eldest grand-daughter, so beautifully said from the altar steps. And another aisle for me to remember now. Faces in the choir stalls, the sturdy shoulders of sons and grandsons supporting the casket before me, Alison clinging to my arm, outside the mocking brightness of the summer afternoon. I slipped her wedding ring on my finger. It is on the hand which steadies this page. A story ended, a wondrous romance. Now the epilogue to life, surplus years to live.

The trees are still in tumult. Driving in from the Tasman a slanting rain has smeared the view. 'There are the tears of things,' said Vergil, hauntingly. How true that half line.

February 5

I am writing again because she has been strangely with me all day. I have kept her little Honda car, and with the empty seat beside me I drove across town through Blockhouse Bay. Her family home occupied the high site of the old blockhouse whence the redcoats watched the Manukau Harbour when those lamentable wars were alive. The traverses of the entrenchments ran round the hilltop garden. We would sit in a summer-house built of the army's timber, and watch the great harbour below.

I drove on to Hillsborough, another harbourside suburb where David has his practice, and on through the green oaks of Cornwall Park on the slopes of Auckland's greatest archaeological monument, One Tree Hill, with the terraced fortifications from the Maoris' Golden Age on the Isthmus, two and three centuries ago . . . She would drive me that way on the first Monday of every month, on which day, from 1974, I have met a large group on the other side of the city for an hour's Bible study. For four years we worked through John's Gospel. She came with me, no longer at the wheel, limping, speechless but serene and beautiful until that November of 1977. The sharp memory rode in the empty seat today. I paused under the oak where we once paused to hear my friend, Malcolm Muggeridge, on the car radio. The spring green became summer green, faded and came again in my year of waiting. It was dark green again this morning and will soon be yellowing.

And I go on, along a route which I cannot abandon, alone. I can say with truth and can say no more, that I carry on as she would wish me to do, doggedly, in pain. I speak to the group without faltering, as I did today, and no one knows that I still see a face to my right among them, eyes fixed, a little anxiously, on mine.

Will that vision ever go? I do not want it to go. Therein is my dilemma. I do not want memory to fade, but memory lies behind my eyes and dims my sight with tears. I serve, and any gift I have with which to serve is God's, but I serve without the lift of the soul, the pure happiness of bygone days – of the Dreamtime, if you will.

But can I do more? I obey, and as Glubose was told by Screwtape, 'our cause was never more in danger', than at such a time – when one of God's creatures, reft, desolated, seemingly abandoned, 'by sheer will-power continues to obey'. That, I tell you, is the only paragraph written which has given me encouragement in this wilderness of anguish. Dear, I have done what was to be done.

February 6

IT is a public holiday, and Peter and David took me walking on the West Coast. We followed a southward path through bush and along the wild walls of the land, such scenery I cannot match in the world. Where the rough path climbed to its highest point over stupendous cliffs, I found a sunny patch of grass in the dense, low scrub, and, desiring solitude, suggested that the others go on, and that we should meet again in two hours at the point where our cliff-edge track had left the wider trail. Left alone, I lay on my back, my face gently shaded by a karaka branch across the high sun. I listened with closed eyes to the eternal monotone of the Tasman surf, far below on the stubborn rocks, and to the million, million leaves talking together as the west wind climbed and brushed the crags. I was in a world of muted sound, aware of every small bird and insect noise, and feeling almost disembodied as I lay in the sun-dappled grass.

I was almost at peace, that peace which some who write hymns and books of devotion, profess so easily to find. My deep wound seemed, in Nature's warmth, to ache a little less, and I thought with a quieter sadness of Cornish coasts, of Scotland's western edge, of Australia across the horizon, where we have heard the moaning of the wave together. Yes, we have known 'sunset and evening star and after that the dark' on Tennyson's Down above the white cliffs of the Isle of Wight. We have pictured that brooding spirit with whom we felt so intimately at one.

Has she 'met her Pilot face to face', now that she

has 'crossed the bar'? Or is it not like that? Half-asleep, I felt time melt. It was like some emancipation from the flesh which it was difficult to hold. Some who have been brought dramatically back from death, speak of such experience. Did she see me bending over her bed, and Alison gripping my hand?

There was something odd about that time on the cliff-top. The two hours went swiftly, as I could wish all my remaining hours would flow by, down the 'ever-rolling stream'. I rose and picked up the lunch packs, which had formed my pillow, and clambered down the track to the rendezvous. I sat on a mossy bank to wait, and suddenly remembered that we had spent the first anniversary of our wedding down in the old boarding-house in Karekare Bay. And we had walked that path from its southern end. We were caught in a deluge of spring rain – fifty years ago. I saw her again, so fresh and beautiful that my wound opened wide. Then, almost uncannily, the two men came into view, her sons, following unwittingly their mother's young footsteps. They are in more ways than one her memorials. Gratitude? Indeed, I am grateful to her for giving them life, to Peter, almost at the cost of her own. I am grateful that I have them by me, men who live as their mother would have them live. It must be my tragic weakness that every memory, even when such gratitude holds its hand, these beautiful possessions of the heart and mind, bring anguish so sharp.

February 7

THIS is Wednesday, the day of her passing. Tomorrow will be the full year, but I cannot escape seven minutes before one o'clock on the middle day of this my Holy Week.

They had moved her to a corner room, from which, had she been conscious, she could have seen, ten miles away, and mauve under the sky, the hillside of thirty years of life. Alison was watching by her when I came in. The Medical School is just across the road and she was often, as a senior student, about the hospital in her white coat.

We sat beside the bed and the still, quiet face. We went out to lunch and returned at one o'clock. A young doctor hurried forward: 'Professor, your wife passed away seven minutes ago.' Another scene, another sentence, 'to remember for years, to remember with tears' . . . While Alison telephoned

I felt her brow grow chill beneath my hands. I kissed her pale lips. So cold. I remembered when I first kissed them, warm and shyly responsive, on January 16, 1925 ... I cannot write more of that afternoon. The page blurs.

.   .   .

'Write about it.' After the Christmas sermon which I commonly give in the Cathedral, I went to the Deanery for a cup of tea. It was difficult to return, but I try to do all I have done before. So she would urge me. In my stall by the pulpit I kept seeing the slow cortège. And how often, in the lingering December twilight, have we gone together over to the lovely old Deanery.

'Why,' I asked John Rymer, 'why do you want me to write about it?' 'To show people some sign-posts,' he answered. I have to this date not seen any in my mist of tears. Perhaps that is my fault. In which of the Narnia stories, does Aslan tell the children to look for four signs as they pursue their mission? They miss them until they have passed by. I, too, have been, perhaps, blind, too preoccupied with the track as I have trudged this valley – 'boots, boots, boots, boots, goin' up and down again ...'

I have obeyed, marching on. I have written, preached, given many the counsel and advice they think I can richly give, alas! I have lectured, taught, and people no doubt set me down as 'victorious' over sorrow! I function on the radio, in the press, as a normal human being, the 'public figure' they all expect me to be. They do not see the broken thing which sheds all disguise when the door shuts. Like Tithonus, 'with what other eyes', I do what I must do.

February 8

THE calendar date. One year ago. The hours have been leaden but full of kindness. In 1958 George Duncan spoke at Keswick of Elijah's vast sorrow, and his flight. He was helped along the way. The 'angel', he suggested, was a peasant woman who did what she could. How many kindly women have done as much for me.

'Under the juniper,' said George Duncan, 'watch for little tokens of God's love.' I have had them all day, the minister at the door, letters in the mail, the gentlest voices on the telephone, and the family. Alison phoned from Napier. Ken, her younger brother, came and spent an hour sitting with me – Ken, so quiet, but who went every evening to see his grandmother over her last weeks ... All is still as I write, a close and heavy night in which it will be hard to sleep. 'The longest day' dies hard.

In this sombre quietude I survey the terrible year, and feel sure there is no healing but only the skilled and more skilled covering of the wound. One can learn to act and spare the world the sight of pain. There it was that poor old Queen Victoria failed – not in her wild grief for Albert, but in her hiding at Windsor with the riff-raff making ribald verse about it all.

February 9

IS that all, then, that I shall be able to say to others, if I ever allow others to read this record of sorrow? I shall write on for two or three more months and hope that, in the stern preoccupations those months will give, that some glimpse may be given of that which is to be, some fragmentary conclusion, a glimmer of hope.

But have I not, all my life, believed and taught that Perfect Love and Perfect Wisdom must combine to produce a Perfect Plan for a life committed to God? I have seen it happen. As a young man did I not see what appeared ultimate disaster in my University career made fruitful and fulfilling beyond all my imagining? The transformation and the gifts it brought called for all my trust, and covered fourteen years. I cannot turn from that conviction now. Principal Edman of Wheaton College, Illinois, once wrote in a book he gave me: 'Never doubt in the darkness what God taught you in the light.' I must exercise myself to remember. Job, I suppose, strove to do this. He was told in the end that God is so immeasurably great that man cannot understand his purposes . . .

I want more than that. And we are offered more in Christ, who died to demonstrate that God is involved in some cosmic process along with man. To be a Christian at all one must believe that to be true, and that all will one day fall into the pattern.

The mind struggles with the thought. I awoke at first light this morning, and hardly yet alert, found a line of Vergil running through my brain. The dying Dido opened her eyes, 'sought the light, and groaned when she had found it' – 'ingemuitque reperta' . . . It was just before six o'clock. It is now nine. I prayed desperately at dawn for 'little tokens of God's love'. I have already had three over the telephone.

*   *   *

The day is done as I sit with the little leather-bound book before me again. Heavy cloud which sometimes comes with an anticyclone has covered the sky all day, putty-coloured, depressing. Utter stillness without a moving leaf, and pressing hard upon me. I react too strongly to weather, and that is true even of two years and more ago, in those now almost unimaginable days of happiness, before the blanket of the dark was spread. I have looked back on what I have written. For whom? Might I harm some? On the other hand, could it be that such frankness might help those who are taunted for their grief, and feel that faith is vain if it does not extinguish agony? After all, when we cry in our desolation: 'My God, my God, why hast thou forsaken me?' we are actually quoting Christ.

KATHLEEN

February 18

IT is nine days since I last wrote. I was dramatically prevented from a comment on the 10th –
the anniversary of the crowded Cathedral, and that
slow cortège ... This hillside is perilous for the
active elderly, with terraces, banks, walls. I rashly
climbed to remove a branch from a copper-beech
and remembered with a pang how, when I cut
three others exactly two years ago, she had appeared on the terrace in front of the dining-room
and begged me to be careful. I climbed down but I
had remembered too late. I set my foot on a loose
stone and was hurled backwards down a steep
shrubbery. I fell across a round rock and crushed in
some back ribs. Three inches to the left might have
meant a crushed spine; a further roll and it would
have been a six-foot drop to the concrete drive and
a fractured skull.

And so there have been painful days in bed sus-
tained by loving neighbours and family. I lie here

still, having narrowly escaped pneumonia, peth-edine-misted days with the empty bed beside me. My deranged thinking has contained the thought that she was spared some of the physical pain of age – only seventy-two. It must have been near the end of '76, after a happy day, that I said as we were driving home: 'Well, if the end to the joy we have known together is soon to come, we have had a full life. And if one of us must be left to the ultimate agony, I hope that it is I who shall carry that burden.' 'That,' she said warmly, 'is real love.' My wish was soon to be granted, and I do accept it as a benediction. I bear her burden, in a vaguely Christ-like way, and it has given my joy, if I may use the word, to embrace what she has been spared.

February 21

DAVID had a dream last night. His mother came to him, it seemed, from the right in a green marble hall. She led him to the statue of a brown lion – Aslan, I suppose, in the imagery of the phantasy – and she spoke of it as a symbol of the strength his manhood was developing. 'You are a dear son,' she said, smiled, as he saw her smile, a week before she died. It was a dream built out of his longing for the wise counsel she had given him since his childhood.

I could wish that she would thus come to me, instead of these drugged nightmares I have had since I hurt myself. It would in some way armour me against the hard, sick shafts of doubt. Yes, I said doubt. It comes in days of weakness. 'Doubt,' I heard our godly professor of anatomy, Kingsley Mortimer, once say, 'is a common experience, but it cannot be a way of life.' I think real faith is prone to it. It is the curse of the academic mind to want evidence, evidence. I can truly say that doubt is not my way of life. The evidence of all I hold to, permeates all my years, but the conflicts of this year, raging through a personality sicklied by melancholy (for so, like Hamlet, I was made) have given me many a torment. I have, lying here on the piled pillows, been driven back to fundamentals – my conviction of a Mind behind Phenomena, my historian's certainty of the Resurrection. And all the love and loveliness, which was my dear one, cannot, cannot pass like air when a heart falters. No, no, life cannot be so absurd. Could an agglomeration of molecules, carbon, oxygen and the rest, produce the pain which has now filled a score of pages in this small notebook? These insensate trees outside the bedroom window, calm in summer sunshine now, can have in truth no more moods than those which wind and weather give them. They speak only to that which is within us, a 'spirit'.

February 22

TODAY is a case in point. This record must be honest or abandoned, and it must contain even days like this. Is it some overhang of drugs from my injury and clotting right leg? Is it the lid of cloud which covers the land again? Is is some 'low' in a healing process? I cannot say, but it has been a day of unrelieved agony. I have lain like Gulliver, bound down by ten thousand tiny threads, unable to rouse myself till this late afternoon. If 'writing about it' is of any use therapeutically, it must be attempted now, but I have so far in these continuing confessions, discovered no path to healing.

I have always been deeply sceptical of the clinical psychologists' 'five stages of grief'. I always doubted that 'time will heal'. We shall see, perhaps. Edward England told me in August, that he thought relief, like our prenatal person, required nine months of gestation. I have waited longer, but from the womb of desolation no newborn life has emerged.

I read again last month Lewis' *A Grief Observed*. It gave me no point of contact. Vanauken's book, named after a word of the same great Christian, simply horrified me. A young wife was tragically dead. Perhaps, said Lewis, it was 'a severe mercy' – Davy was taken before, with passing years, love, once warm, might grow cold, or, as somebody says, before it could invade the love of God. I do not know a God like that.

We had half a century. I loved those soft brown eyes when she was sixteen and I eighteen. Their lenses are now giving someone clearer sight. I hated to think of their scalpels over her but knew she would want such fragments to be of use.

'A severe mercy' – what mercy can I find in my utter loneliness? None, none. I have prayed all day for Socrates' 'sure word of God', but the cloud cover is still putty-grey. Perhaps others might find wondering alleviation in my confession, those poor folk who think Christian leaders, as they think I am, are somehow armoured as they are not. 'Of course, you have other resources,' said the man across the counter in the bank, thinking to spare me the offer of pity. A neighbour on the other hill said the same on the telephone today. So little do they understand. I met a bewildered negative last night when I asked a man whether he thought much of the past ...

The past, the blessed past, dear God, I never forget it, its glory and agony combined. We stood together all those years facing trouble, stress, conflict, side by side and shocking their assault – as well as enjoying together all the peace, love, fulfilment, interest and wide adventure of a crowded life. She covered me with her deft weaponry, and shared the wounds as well as the victories. I know that, if she could, she would be with me in this last fight of all, but I hear no clink of steel beside me, as I always did, none. I seem so terrifyingly alone. Sorry pages are these, but have they somehow purged a little of today's despair, and brought a modicum of courage back? John Laird reminded me of James Barrie's inaugural address on courage at St. Andrews, and his quotation:

> 'I am hurt,' said Sir Andrew Barton,
> 'I am wounded, but not yet slain,
> I'll lay me down and bleed awhile,
> Then rise and fight again.'

How I have striven over a year of ferocious activity, writing, broadcasting, to the tune of a million words, to be up on my feet sword swinging again, but like Cyrano in that last scene, weapon bare and his back against a tree, I have felt the haemorrhage continue, and unless the wound is soon staunched I do not know what the next months will bring. And I have this task ahead of leading a large party to the Middle East and Europe. I cannot fail them, and the event begins to build a wall across the year, over which I cannot see. Could it be 'still waters', that spread on the other side?

February 24

THE body's pain has eased, and strangely I feel strengthened in the spirit's fight. Medication, I think, can play havoc with the mind. I have banished analgesics and have even achieved a little writing, that sporadic relief of last year. I am up on my knees again, sword out and prepared to fight.

February 25

SUNDAY afternoon again, three weeks since I began this threne, and I am beaten to the ground to bleed again. The house itself is a part of my defeat. We shared its beauty here on the hillside at the forest's edge, and its every room echoes with her words and her footsteps, quick on the stair when I arrived home. The carpets she chose are under my feet, shrubs she planted are in the borders. I open a drawer, and there lie things set in order by her hands, her chair is by the fireplace, here in my long library.

What if I were to move house? Edward England warned me. In circumstances like mine, he had been disposed to do so, but was checked by Toffler's *Future Shock*. Why add to the shock of a devastating blow? He was right. Anyway, I would rather have the pain of memory than contrived forgetfulness. I want, want to remember, not in self-torture, but because everything she was is a part of me, and if any detail dies, that is my own death. All I can wish is that some elusive tenderness, even joy might invade that lifelong memory, that the anguish, almost physical might be leached from it.

I have been to Peter's home for lunch and have thought much of the simple faith of my grandson, John. It helped in today's battle in a way that words more sophisticated in theology or 'counselling' fail to do. I know those answers, alas!

February 26

BOTH of my good friends who urged me to this task of writing, overestimating me, as friends do, had in mind that I would say something useful. I wonder whether much of what I have so far confessed can give hope or relief to any who, like me, have been so beaten down in battle. I have more than once heard in the mind's recesses the old Sankey dirge: 'Go bury thy sorrow, the world has its share . . .'

It comes to my mind, however, that I can say

something of use. I have set myself a date for renewed physical normality – this sunny Monday, in
fact. After a strange battle of will, I forced myself to
rise early and went to the gymnasium where, under
that fine Christian, Don Oliver, our Olympic
champion weightlifter, I have been training my
legs for next month's clambering over archaeological sites. My broken ribs caused lamentable
suspension of these exercises. I found the task too
demanding and a bayonet was twisting under my
right ribs. But it did make me move. I shall lecture
at Bible College tomorrow. I shall record some talks
for Radio N.Z. on Wednesday. After long torpidity,
I shall write some pages for the Bible Handbook,
taking shape on my desk. I am, in a word, resuming
last year's active therapy, which February's agonising anniversary and the horrible accident were
filching away. Be normal even if normality has its
measure of pretence, I have told myself. Work,
work hard. No hard work ever harmed a man, and
in loneliness, in life's evening, what matters it if
hard work should do damage? Better shine in use
than rust unburnished.

I know, after such resolve, I feel calmer as the
last sunlight filters through the trees. I am one day
nearer reunion, and, if I have any useful work to do,
I know that Kath would want me to turn to it with
a will. In the long years she endured much loneliness to promote my work; I wish that I had told

her more often that I knew and appreciated her self-sacrifice ... Here comes the first star – 'and after that the dark ... and there shall be no moaning of the bar when I embark ...'

March 1

A MORE tranquil month, I trust. I cling to the thought that February, in addition to its traumatic dates, may have been distorted by physical pain, with too much time in bed to think, think ... I have declared myself recovered, disregarding the remnants of that bayonet in my back. I have been into the city and unfalteringly recorded those radio talks, resuming the familiar dichotomy of last year whereby, a broken spirit in private, I functioned in public with convincing normality. No doubt my audiences and listening public thought how 'victoriously' I had vanquished sorrow. So little do we know our fellow-men, and what goes on in the secret places of the soul ...

I observe that Vanauken's book, *A Severe*

Mercy, is marked as 'the book of the year', in a large American publication. I was awake in the night thinking about it. I cannot give a clear explanation why that tale of young, married love was so drastically ended, in the same manner in which, so far, I see no clear purpose or reason for my own desolation. I can only say that it is honest to recognise a mystery, and see inexplicable sorrow for what it is.

Grief and groping are not sin. There is no divine command to be jolly. Candide and Mark Tapley are equally irritating, and although I am in no way likening Lewis' 'explanation' of the poor girl's death to the words of either, I maintain that it is of little use to follow such wraiths of comfort in such a fog of grief. Perhaps, with less than justice, I think of Binyon's poem:

They shall grow not old as we that are left grow old,
Age shall not weary them, nor the years condemn.

Congratulations, in a word , you have escaped arthritic old age in one searing blast of shrapnel in the tangled wire. But who am I to be critical of Lewis who thus gave a young man comfort?

For my part, I know that I am in the hands of a wise and loving God. I have taught, and still believe that the fact implies a purpose interwoven in the fabric of life. God, none the less, does not expect me to twist my mind to discover a pattern, where, too close to the tapestry, I cannot yet trace it. I say again that, since one of us had to face it, it is satisfaction to be the one chosen to bear it, and that it is I, and not she, who am left, cross-laden to trudge this Via Dolorosa.

March 7

IT is almost a week since I last wrote – a pain-wracked time, with damaged ribs taking their leisure to heal. I have been busy with the postponed tasks of life and have observed with a sombre wonder, the dichotomy of which I spoke – the functioning person and the mask which hides the quiet desperation. I go out with friends, I speak here and there, but always in the nether levels of my mind is the thought of that awful moment when I shall reach home, put the key in the door, and feel the dull wave of emptiness flow out to meet me, embrace and overwhelm.

I have found in a drawer between our beds a slip

of paper on which she had written a prayer of the Rev. E. F. Farr. It was on faded paper, and obviously written years ago, put aside to serve, I suppose, her own moment of need, that which, thank God, I bear for her. The words run: 'Father we pray for all lonely people, especially those who, coming home to an empty house, stand at the door hesitant and afraid to enter. May all who stand in a doorway with fear in their hearts, like the two on the Emmaus Road, ask the Living One in. Then, by his grace, may they find that in loneliness they are never alone, and that he peoples empty rooms with his presence.' So, dear God, I would do. It is a pale, dull afternoon. It will be heavy night when I return home later. Soften that moment.

March 8

I HAVE been haunted all day by the last lines of a hymn:

> *. . . Bringing all my burdens,*

KATHLEEN

Sorrow, sin and care;
At thy feet I lay them,
And I leave them there.

The last five words have turned me often to prayer.
My sorrow? Can God turn it into something beautiful and fruitful? My sin? I explore corners of my life
in these days of self-searching, and know that, of all
my faults, there is not one for which I am not ready
to ask forgiveness or expose to ruthless probing (if
God can ever be called 'ruthless'). Care? To leave
this and the rest at Christ's feet, requires the deepest
act of faith. Perhaps, in a more outreaching prayer-
life, I am to discover some new tract of understanding.

I have wondered about the most difficult of the
Beatitudes. Those who mourn are called blessed –
'for they shall be comforted'. I am sure that the
promise cannot mean a mere dulling of pain. I
think the literal meaning of the Greek verb must
tell the true story. It says: '. . . they shall be called
alongside.' Of whom? Surely God himself. I can
truly say that I have sought that intimacy as never
before, as Job put it, 'to draw near to his dwelling',
and plead my case. I can draw a measure of relief
from the thought that he will one day, in such close-
ness, teach me the meaning of tears, and make
clear, I trust in joy, what he has sought of me in the
abysm of this awful experience. Perhaps it is only in

this reach of trust that I take all, 'and leave them there'.

March 10

TIME is puzzling. These sixteen months I have lived here without her in a house crammed with memories, seem longer than the thirty-two years of blessed fellowship in the home we built and enjoyed so richly together. I look to dates and anniversaries, and I suppose we master and control time in so far as we thus divide it. I hold fast to the thought that April 2, when I take that large party abroad, will be a sort of milestone. Tremendous preoccupations, at least by day, will fill my mind. Will such activity perhaps interrupt and fill some obstinate neuronic channels and circuits in the brain? And then, such is the form of my imagination, the intervening three weeks become an arid wilderness, a hot veld, over which, like Kipling's Boer War soldier, I march with grim and desperate doggedness. I watch the marching column:

KATHLEEN

*... Boots, boots, boots, boots, movin' up and
down again,*

. . . .

*Men, men, men, men, men go mad with
watchin' 'em,*

. . . .

*Count count, count, count, the bullets in
the bandoliers,*

. . . .

Oh, my God, keep me from goin' lunatic,

There's no discharge in the war.

It is like that – all, all, all, all along the path of
Tsalmaveth, the Valley of the Shadow of Death.
And still I have no message to give, no lesson
learned – save it be this: 'Press on, on, on, on, with
the boots, boots, boots, boots moving up and down
again ...' in truth our marching column is long,
small comfort it is that others suffer too, and endure
what I endure. I often look at the dozen or the score
in each day's newspaper and feel a brotherhood ...
Tennyson knew, or feared:

Tears of the widower when he sees
  A late-lost form that sleep reveals,
  And moves his doubtful arms, and feels
Her place is empty, fall like these.

Yes, mortally long seem the three weeks ahead. Is it that I hope half unconsciously for some insight or revelation in retracing paths we shared?

March 12

PETER'S birthday, her elder son. How well I remember that anxious thirty-six hours in which she strove to give him birth, a shocking travail which almost cost her precious life, an ordeal borne with that quiet and steadfast courage which was always part of her. She would have used it to face life had she survived me.

But let me pause and consider. Can courage be measured and assessed by what we feel in the broken heart, and the silent night, or has it a place too in the building of the façade to cover and screen our reality?

There was half a page about me in the weekend newspaper. A journalist of standing, had condensed into it a whole morning's talk, and the adjective he used of me, dear God, was 'zestful' – of me who

trudge, trudge, 'boots, boots . . .'! But if I am giving
that impression to a shrewd and clever man, am I
not doing all that God and man can expect of me,
and not darkening others with the murk of my un-
ending sorrow? I know well enough that it is not
possible to hide my wounded self from my family.
It causes me pain that I undoubtedly distress them,
but I record the journalist's word: 'Zestful, fit, with
a passion for travel.' I am glad that those who look
to me to lead them do not realise how I dread the
task. I covet a salutary preoccupation, but will I not
be conscious, from Singapore to Los Angeles, that,
on all those other occasions of leadership which have
enlivened my retirement, it was two of us who
shared the task? Wise she was, gracious, gentle, and
immediately beloved by all who went with us.
'Zestful' – alas!

March 15

BOOTS, boots, boots ... Just the same, but
has the landscape grown a little brighter,
msasa glowing in the veld? I cannot remember

praying with more intensity than I did one day earlier this week. I do not believe that God measures the passion of our supplication, and so doles out his answer, but two years ago, with this ordeal beginning to take shape, in the very spot by Galilee where he said the words, I sat under a magnolia and heard distantly someone reading the Sermon on the Mount. I thought of the literal rendering as the boy's voice read on: 'Keep on praying, keep on asking . . .' I seemed to sense a promise that she would not die. She died, she died.

I seem to be today at some climax of tears and distress. Is it an Emmaus Road and not a Via Dolorosa which I tread? It was in May 1977, that we walked that cobbled Roman road together for the last time. I found today a small photograph someone had sent me. I was reading the Emmaus story from my Greek Testament, and she sat with those who listened in her blue hat. I wish I knew what was going on in her dear mind, already muted by the invading Thing . . .

On that road they walked into the dazzle of the setting sun, and did not recognise the One who joined them. Even when they stopped, their eyes still blinded by the red sun dropping to the Mediterranean, curiously they did not discern him. Am I thus blinded? I am trudging west also. The shadows lengthen behind me. Is it possible that I am so dazed by my grief that I do not sense the Presence, he who is still teaching in the very Scriptures of my life's experience, 'the things concerning himself'? If so, then let my eyes be opened. And does that give hope for the lifting of the cloud? Writing is a little easier. Some of the lethargy, which has plagued two months, has gone. Let it continue.

March 16

I HAVE thought much of that strange experience on the Mount. I remember little of that few weeks abroad. They were too loaded with anxiety, but the morning on the slope under the little octagonal basilica remains vivid. Kath was brave, her usual tranquil courage moving her, when she came on that expedition, conscious of her stumbling words. She always met difficulties and duties face to face, but was not able this time to fulfil the tasks of leadership and ministry which were always her strong and gracious function among the women of the party.

On that occasion she remained with her

unuttered thoughts upon the bus, when we visited the hillside of Christ's Beatitudes. It is a lovely place above the Tabgha Vale. From a seat on a crumbling stone wall under the magnolia, I could look over the silver shield of Galilee under a vast blue bowl of sky. The mauve hills of the Golan walled the east. I might have been sitting where Christ sat as he spoke to those prepared to climb and hear him. I bowed in an agony of supplication: 'Dear God, let this cup pass from me, spare her in Christ's name, spare her.'

Then I heard those words of which I wrote yesterday, as though Someone said: 'Be silent and listen to me.' 'Keep on asking . . .' I grasped those words, stronger in the Greek text than in most of the translations. I laid hold of them with both hands. She would get better, and we should begin to live again, death once more defeated. I long held to the conviction that such was God's answer. But she died, she died, in spite of that prayer, and the true faith in which I held it. Where then was God's promise? I shall have a rendezvous with God in that same place next month, like Habakkuk, 'get me to my watchtower and see what he will say to me.'

But I think I know already what he will say. He stilled my anguished prayer that morning, and bade me listen because he was about to allow me to face that which I dreaded more than death – the loss of one supremely loved. He was telling me to go on praying, seeking, clamouring for light, until the time when I shall see with drier eyes what he had and has in mind to do to my life, to penetrate, perhaps, new corners of my being and lead to some deeper understanding, some nobler living.

At my age? I was a young man when I added a verse to that familiar hymn: 'Just as I am, young strong and free . . .' The new verse runs:

> *Just as I am though youth is past,*
> *And the leaves are dry in the autumn blast,*
> *Though few be the years I can give – at last,*
> *O Lamb of God, I come.*

Like many words I have uttered in the course of my life, I am now called upon to turn those words into the stuff of reality in a new passion of surrender. I have made that surrender, though I feel no uplift of the soul. I trudge on, back to the magnolia. Perhaps he will tell me there.

E. M. BLAIKLOCK

March 17

I CAME across a note of William Barclay on Revelation 4: 'Out of sorrow, can come bitterness and resentment, but sorrow can produce a faith, and a peace, and a new song.' I am not bitter, only stricken. I am not resentful, because to resent what God has permitted, could only be for me a denial of the reality of God. But I have yet found no new depth of faith, small peace, and certainly no new song to sing. What are the words? . . . 'washed wondrously with sorrow . . .'? I think I do experience a certain cleansing, a new tenderness of conscience, a deeper pain over failure, that might not have come to me save for this tramping in the gloom.

With all my heart I could wish Barclay's words to prove true for me. Was he writing from real experience? Did he know? Nothing would I desire more than to say those words and set my seal to them, this battle won, this quest accomplished, the

door on which I keep knocking opened to a new
Narnia of meaning –

> *Lo, all my heart's field red and torn,*
> *And thou wilt bring the young green corn,*
> *And when the field is fresh and fair,*
> *Thy blessed feet shall glitter there,*
> *And we will walk the weeded field*
> *And tell the harvest's golden yield,*
> *The corn that makes the holy bread*
> *By which the soul of man is fed,*
> *The holy bread, the food unpriced,*
> *Thy everlasting mercy, Christ.*

No harvest yet, but the winter ploughing with the
muddy share jarring on many an unsuspected
stone. But the poetry and Scripture with which I
have ever filled my mind, spill out thus to challenge,
daunt, or move elusive hope.

March 18

I AM writing late tonight. It is another of those wild nights of fearsome wind which always disturb me. More now, for the roaring trees will be forever linked with the late November day when she stumbled out of my life. It is one of those times of lonely memory which always bow my spirit down. Sheer will, as that passage from *The Screwtape Letters* has it, becomes heavily involved at such times. It took all I could summon up of determination to sit at the table and make myself continue writing about Acts. I am in the dining-room where the raging of the trees is less apparent than in my library.

As I look up she smiles down on me from a photograph on the wall. It was a press photograph taken at Government House when I was invested with the OBE five years ago. A beautiful smile. I think she approves. If only I knew that she knows. I have written now some four thousand words and begin to tire.

March 20

I THINK I tired myself too much last night, and I failed to sleep. Perhaps today has been reaction – a veritable Vale of Tears. I gave two lectures at Bible College, and I think I taught and spoke without apparent stress. It was when I entered the empty house in the early afternoon that the desolation of life without her enveloped me like a shroud. If anyone ever reads this it will be perhaps to despise my frailty, rather than to understand how, after fifty-eight weeks, I can still sob and call to her. The grief will not abate, nor transform itself, though in truth I have offered it to God for such an alchemy. What more must I learn? Dear God, if there are deeper lessons awaiting, let me learn them soon and depart.

March 21

A PRAYER has come my way which I must at all costs learn to pray: 'Take, O Lord, and receive all my liberty, my memory, my understanding and all my will. All I have and possess, it is thine. To thee, O Lord, I return it. Dispose of it according to thy will. Give me thy love and grace for that is sufficient for me.' Therein, I suppose, is the answer to yesterday's lamentable defeat. Thus, perhaps can memory become a stimulus to do always as she would wish me to do. Thus, to be sure, I can conquer the paralysis of will which keeps me pinned in her chair by the window, when I know that a positive task awaits me. I am not free to hope that life be shortened and reunion accelerated. God help me, for I mean it, I mean it . . .

March 22

SHE had prepared herself for the lot that is mine, spurred to do so by the illnesses which for all the strength I now have, marked the first half of our married life. In her desk there are two drawers full of notes and addresses she gave. It always cost her much to speak, but she did it brilliantly. I found a slip of paper on which she had written: 'The last task of all is to put away self-pity, learn to enjoy loneliness, to get rid of possessions, and to live for others.'

I can say that I have been trying to do some of that, but if loneliness is being without her, how can I ever enjoy that? And, tell me, when and where does grief become self-pity? Early enough, I imagine, in the censorious minds of those who have not learned with Paul to 'weep with those that weep'.

Oscar Wilde had to confess in that moving testament, *De Profundis*, that he had found the spectacle of unhappiness and pain of any sort repugnant. In the end he was obliged to drink the last dregs of it, mixed with tears, from a tin prison mug. 'Go bury your sorrow', or some will dissect it like a corpse. I think Kath had foreseen that when she wrote those words, when over twenty-five years ago I lay at the Edge of Beyond for four vanished days after a partial gastrectomy.

How vividly I remember when I slipped one day out of bed and, clutching my stitched abdomen, shuffled to a little room across the corridor where there was a telephone. I dialled our number and have always heard the cry of delight: 'Life begins again,' she said. For me there is no new beginning, only left-over years to live. Would I go back, if that were possible, and live all those together years again? A thousand times, whatever another life may hold.

I read in Boothby's memoirs of a talk with Churchill. 'Is life worth living?' asked Boothby. 'Once,' said the Old Man. Could I have foreseen in all sharp detail the bitter pain which chills this evening, I should still have chosen the path I took. Our life was too perfect, the Greeks would say, and jealous heaven hurled its javelin. Not so for the Christian, surely, only the sparks flying upwards.

I am writing these musings down because it has been a hard day, murky with the dun skies of this appalling autumn. I have been writing steadily, but seeking excuses to use the telephone for little other reason than to hear a voice. The faint hope lies in me that some day, as any day can do, may bring some Annunciation, some Theophany to transform and bring gladness. Such alleviation lies, I know in God's sovereign will, but I go tramping on meanwhile, looking for 'the sign posts'. Soon I must take my large party abroad including David, Jean, Peter's wife, and Anne. 'Serving others,' of Kath's note? Surely. I can claim that measure of obedience.

March 27

THESE five days have been a featureless landscape and the marching hard, with many a stone to stumble on, and few rough places made plain. With set teeth I have tramped on.

Two senior nuns, long years ago my students, visited me on Sunday. They told me that they daily pray for me, and I saw a glimmer of light. Is it a 'signpost' when someone can say: 'I shall leave others to pray for me. Meanwhile I shall pray for others' – and there is another laid this day upon my heart.

March 28

EARLY today, as I drove home from the gymnasium where I make myself go once a week for a physical 'workout', I thought again of the mask I wear. I had guests last night, and I am sure that my conversation, animated at times, convinced them of my restoration. It must follow that always, when I have seen the bereaved function in public with seeming normality, I look only at a screen, a façade. My guests gone, the tide rolled back, billow on billow over me. So must it be with others. Long exposure to the listening audience, I suppose, gives me this facility. And so I have learned a little of others and gained a facet of understanding. Like Ezekiel, I have 'sat where they sat', and been 'astonished'.

But it is so difficult to postulate of others what is

true of oneself. The psychologists warn against 'self-equation'. For example, I have never been able to grasp C. S. Lewis' point when he likens grief to fear. But I do grant this – grief demoralises and spills into fear. Hence today's strong blast of apprehension over the immense responsibilities I assume next week in taking sixty-five people to Israel, Turkey, Greece and the rest. I can even trace it crookedly to the depression which never lies far away from the loneliness of grief. I can even identify a source. I am using her suitcase and packing, for the first time, alone. I found she had put aside some items of clothing – not hers but mine – against such an occasion.

I shall never know how much she knew. It was part of her torment that, silenced by this dread glioma, she could not say how much she knew. Her wavering fingers could not write. She must have known that she was dying, and have guessed that I would seek some therapeutic preoccupation in travelling again. I bowed over the carefully selected undergarments and dissolved into tears beyond control. Does she know now? Would she could make her presence felt in the Garden Tomb or over Galilee.

E. M. BLAIKLOCK

April 2

THE DC-10 is high over the Tasman now.
Poignantly there is an empty seat beside me.
Her suitcase is stowed below. Her wedding ring
goes abroad again – on my finger now, a pledge in
more ways than one.

We flew in brilliant sun over our familiar hills. It
was painful to think of the empty house below,
a home no longer, only rooms. But here, in this
remote environment, I sense a strange quietness. I
can understand a widower holding battle in con-
tempt, and doing heroic deeds because he has no
one for whom he really needs to go on living.

I wonder whether, when I return, the door I
unlock will open more than the front hall . . . And
now we are in the steamy heat of Singapore. It is
still April 2, thanks to a long retarding of the clock.
I am alone in the big hotel. Double room. One
empty bed. Something seems bent on reminding
me.

The film they put on in the cabin this afternoon began in a graveyard with a man, a young man, burying his wife. It was quite uncannily calculated to hurt me. He flung himself into work, until, after eighteen months, well-meaning friends tried to persuade him to 'clock in with life' again. I jerked the earphones out, and closed my misted eyes.

April 3

DAVID tells me he watched the film to the end. The man could not forget his wife, and an attempt to form a new attachment foundered on the fact. But in the midst of such fumbling he discovered a new relationship with his parents – exactly the third point in Kath's recipe in her desk – 'learn to live for others'. The message of the film was: 'Only the living need the living.'

I could not sleep last night, in spite of putting the light out at three a.m., New Zealand time. Those words had stirred me too deeply. Does she no longer need me, when, dear God, I need her so? She needed me, as I needed her for a full half-century. She gave much that I would never have elsewhere found – a sensitivity to others' feelings, a steadying hand on hot reactions, a passion for order, forethought and efficiency. And, indeed, she needed me. I first found her, a mere girl, in a state of shock, abruptly brought to New Zealand from a happy and fulfilling school-life in England. She was wounded by her parents' thoughtless uprooting, silent and withdrawn. She loved me from the very first, and the brash confidence which, for a few years, was a feature of my youth, lifted her to confidence and happiness. This is how the perfect harmony in which we lived found genesis.

Illogically, unreasonably perhaps, I cannot bear the thought that she no longer needs me, however deeply ingrained in me are the qualities she, and she only, brought to life in my personality. She lives in me. I catch myself asking her, in some corner of my mind, what I should do, here, there. What sort of other life, I asked myself, as I tossed and turned, can it be in which she no longer needs me? And this leaves me blindly groping, reaching in desperation for the assurance they profess, who 'feel their loved ones always near them'.

Then, of course, my ravaged mind, clicking its computer circuits, begins to throw upon the screen, the poetry with which it is stocked – Rupert Brooke's underlining in his Aristophanes: 'The dead cannot answer though you call them thrice'; or Euripides, which she has heard me read aloud in their lovely Greek in the Epidauros theatre:

> *If any far off state there be,*
> *Dearer to life than mortality,*
> *The hand of death hath hold thereof,*
> *And mists are under and mists above . . .*

Some circuits are shorted by weariness and depression. The computer less readily throws up lines more confident:

> *Thou wilt not leave us in the dust,*
> *Thou madest man, he knows not why,*
> *He thinks he was not made to die,*
> *And thou hast made him thou art just . . .*

No, I cannot believe that the wonder of conscious life is a ghastly joke played by no one on everyone. She must be living. Over that hour when Alison and I last saw her, sixty mortal weeks tomorrow, she was visibly alive, deeply comatose, but looking as I often saw her when I crept out to make morning tea. That was at noon. An hour later when, after the young house-surgeon's words, we burst into the small white room, she had strangely altered. As the smooth brow chilled under my hand I knew that she, my own Kathleen, was departed, gone – somewhere. Earth does not, cannot contain the darkness of the contrary thought.

Singapore was stirring to life beneath the high windows when I finally awoke from a fitful, final doze. She must need me still, though how that can chime with felicity, I do not know. Must felicity be painless? It was not so for Christ.

April 4

I THOUGHT more clearly about it in the light of day, and of course, the answer is obvious. She cannot longer need me to give her strength and confidence, as she no longer needs me to lift the suitcase yonder. She is no longer conscious of weakness, or the things which once daunted and hurt her. She is beyond such earth-bound frailties. It must also be realised that our relationship will be of quite another sort, different but deeper. Here my mind protests, because I want no other relationship than the perfect one we had. To be sure, 'eye has not seen, nor ear heard, nor has anyone in the ultimate depths of his being, understood what God has in store for those who love him'. My tired mind will not think beyond that point.

April 5

I SLID the window back at first break of day to watch the steely level of Galilee grow gold as the sun topped the Golan Heights. I could see the hotel of two years ago. Was it an illusion born of memory and longing, or did a distant figure appear on that high balcony where our room was? She loved to watch the glory of the day spread across the lake. I came in, and slid the door back again. The view had misted in my eyes.

But I kept my rendezvous with God this morning by the magnolia. I sat upon the same wall, and tried to ask God what he meant by telling me to go on asking, seeking, knocking. I was unable to do anything but stammer the question. David came and sat with me as he did two years ago. How deep was her distress, I wonder, as she lingered in the bus, unable to summon resolution to see again the lovely place she had more than once sought and savoured? Those deadly, subtle fingers were creeping cell by cell across her brain, even on the hill where the Lord of Life once spoke.

David found words which eluded me, and prayed. Then we looked along the wall to the place where the boy had sat reading the Sermon as I wrote on March 16. Two of our party were there, bowed in tears. 'There,' said David quietly, 'are two who understand,' and I remembered the tragic death of their son. We got up and went to them to mingle prayers and tears. Perhaps that is all God wishes to say to me at this time. He interrupted me again: 'Share it, let it make you tender. Weep with those that weep.' If, as she says, Alison finds it more easy to do just this, than to rejoice with the rejoicing, then so do I, and I have always so felt.

God, then, has only reaffirmed as he did to stricken John Baptist. I must carry comfort, and so fulfil a role for Christ more gently and with understanding than I might have done without this visitation. Had she been with me and not her son, we still might have done together what he and I did today, and seek, by our fellowship, to take alleviation to those in pain. Perhaps God speaks as slowly as, to our time-fettered minds, he sometimes seems to act, but that was all he had to say to me at our rendezvous above the level lake.

KATHLEEN

Sitting, an hour later, on a log by the Church of Peter's Secrecy, I asked myself whether I would accept the comfort full forgetfulness might bring. No. I would not. If all my memories quiver with the grief I feel, I would rather pay that price for them than have them taken from me. I cannot ask for power to forget, but I can ask for greater courage to remember.

If that urge today to help another was all God had to say, I take hope from the fact that I immediately obeyed. I cherished hope when I came abroad that change of scene might in some way transform. I might better have remembered Horace: 'They change their skies but not their mind who rush off overseas.' It continues as at home. I do my work, and talk of a thousand things from the front of the bus, literature, history, life. I am not a dull companion at table. Then I return to my room at night, walk past her suitcase, look at the Paschal moon silver on the lake, and choke on a sob.

It was her view. She used it in apt illustration in her last address – a talk to women in a Melbourne church in March 1977. There is a girl from Melbourne with us here in Tiberias because of that address. I have it on a tape, and can pick the small, sinister stumbling on words.

E. M. BLAIKLOCK

April 10

THIS record is no fiction. To say less or to say more than the truth; to level out the undulations of the mind, to lop the peaks or exalt the valleys, would destroy the value of anything I might say. I say this lest some weary of me as people do. But today, if the Valley of the Shadow has its deeper crevasses, I have found one and groped through it. It began with an early visit to the Garden Tomb on the Nablus Road, a place we visited together in the sharp, dawn air, fifteen years ago. We walked down from Saint George's Hostel and stood inside the cool tomb in the half-light, which Peter and John saw. We prayed for the family, each member of whom was ever on her careful heart, and walked arm-in-arm in silence – that silence which was our profoundest, wordless fellowship.

I said yesterday that if there was a choice between painful memory and calm forgetfulness, I would choose memory and pay the price. Today's price was a heavy one. All day the flood of tears has pressed hard behind my eyes, and I hope I have not been too obviously stricken for concealment. I went alone deliberately this afternoon through Yad Vashem in a state of horror over the hideous sufferings of Jewry. No one saw my sobbing exit into the sunlight. I sent the party alone into the Shrine of the Book, and reached the bedroom before the storm within me burst.

I had thought that this land of Israel might steady my feet a little on the path. It has torn my wounded spirit wide open instead, and made me despair of finding the tranquillity I so desperately seek. There is only that intense and almost frightening longing to be with her. If God has told me that my saving, and ultimately healing task, is to give my life for others, then he must soon give me stronger enablement. And yet it was in this city that Christ suffered beyond imagining for me. I tread his very Way of Pain, and try tight-lipped not to cry: 'My God, my God, why have you forsaken me?'

'Go on asking, go on knocking . . .' I do, until my voice is hoarse and my knuckles bleed. There must, must be a fuller richer answer than I have yet had revealed.

April 11

WE were just past the Jabbok Gorge, a darker cleft in the mauve hills across the Jordan, when a loud report startled us. I looked instinctively up the bouldered slope to the right, expecting to see some running figure or hanging puff of smoke, but it was no more than a burst tyre.

While repairs were made, I walked a few yards back along the road and looked across at the historic ravine. It is, I think, David's Valley of the Shadow of Death. In his retreat from rebel Absalom, spiritually recorded, I am sure, from Psalm 2 to Psalm 6, David, having struggled north-east across the Judaean hills and Jordan's Zor, or jungle – the 'swellings of Jordan' – spent a grim night in that cleft. Sensitive to history, he thought of Jacob's wrestling. Sensitive as acutely to landscape, he lapsed there into the renewed agony of the sixth psalm.

No one of those who stood and watched the

changing of the tyre, knew why I stared so intently at the dark shadow of the valley's mouth in the Jordanian hills. It seemed to melt into some landscape of the mind. She went that way, stumbling along the back path, past my library chimney, and I know not up what rockstrewn vale of silence, through what untold distress, until February 8. And I, back in time and place, was left like Jacob wrestling by the river's edge with the Guardian of the Land. She has emerged into the quiet Oberland of Mahanaim where the psalmist, welcomed by Barzillai, could make Psalm 23 for his shepherd host.

That upland green is far away, as I struggle up the gorge, but let me be grateful for my Barzillais who have refused to wait, but come down the valley with what sustenance they could carry to me in the dark. My friends and family have been wondrous dear.

E. M. BLAIKLOCK

April 13

GOOD FRIDAY, and perhaps the nineteen hundred and fiftieth anniversary of the crucifixion. Istanbul is a strange and sinister place in which to spend it – in bitter cold and under a loaded sky. We were here with Alison exactly seven years ago, and this tenth-floor room in the big, new hotel must occupy the very airspace of the room we had in the old hotel of '72 with the Bosphorus below, and the black Russian ships passing ... While the others wandered in the bazaar, I elected to sit for an hour in the bus, parked by the door of Saint Sophia.

I thought of the name, 'Holy Wisdom', and watched the crowds – dour Germans, chattering French, impassive Japanese, camera-draped Americans. I was alone with God. Subdued in spirit I counted the blessings of life, a whole rosary of them – that I can sit, as few others can, in sight of the great minarets and feel the living pulse of three thousand years of history, a oneness with the race born of a lifetime's teaching of the classics, that, until now, I have been able to trace a most blessed pattern in my whole experience – surely the threads are not, thus late, broken? I gave thanks for Christ, on this day done to death for me.

And with eyes which dimmed the crocus-blazing flower beds, I gave thanks for the long years she was with me. Empires have risen and fallen in less time than that. Athens' 'Fifty Years', was shorter time than that through which she was a moulding and subduing influence for good in all my life.

In a flash of memory I saw her with Alison entering the great cathedral beside me, wearing the brown check overcoat she for some reason kept for travel overseas. Was it a message to me, by which she thwarted her silence, that she put it on that day of her departure? I lifted her helpless right arm into the sleeve and she looked at me. And I can see her back as she limped along that path. Did she try to say: 'I leave home alone this last time. Come when he calls you?' Was it? Oh, my God, I have only now seen what she tried to say.

April 15

EASTER SUNDAY, and I suppose the strangest Resurrection Day I have ever spent. We followed the Sea of Marmora to Gallipoli, the long Peninsula of Death, and wandered for an hour or two among the four thousand graves which mark that ghastly battlefield. All the serried crosses of the Anzacs stood above the dust of some I remembered marching away when I was a boy at school. They still lie in alien soil.

Christ's grave was empty.

We held a small memorial service at Chunuk Bair and the Turkish driver stood with me. He gave me a white and a golden pebble, and took two just like them, which he put in his pocket. Mine are on my library mantelpiece. The two armies, each by each at peace.

I traversed in mind that night again the arguments which, as an historian, I advance for Christ's rising from the dead, and found them as compelling and persuasive as I always do. If he lives, Kath lives, more really than those seven years ago, when she occupied with me the room opposite, in this old hotel in Cannakale, and Alison was down the corridor.

And if he truly rose, nothing really matters but this pain of waiting. The rising of Christ from the Dark Realm is the final surety, as Paul told the Corinthians, that we too shall rise. Otherwise Omar's question remains without an answer:

Strange, is it not? – that of the thousands who,
Before us passed that door of darkness through,
None should return to tell us of the road,
Which to discover we must travel too . . .

One did, and I am sure of it, and so this shadowed life I live is not darkness to the core. Why then, it might be asked, do I not rest in my assurance of historical truth? Do not press that question. It exposes too obviously my weakness. But ask this – could a mere agglomeration of carbon, hydrogen, oxygen and the rest, which is all I am, if there is not Something Else, quiver with the agony I know? Yes, says an unquenchable whisper – when you shot the myna which was cruelly emptying the starling nest of its bloodstained young, did not its mate dive screaming over the body? It is not the same. That bereaved bird had no words for grief, sorrow, desolation, no self-conscious and complicated misery. Some inbuilt pattern of neurones was disrupted in its tiny computer brain. I cannot scream it all away and go forgetfully.

April 16

STANDING on Pergamum's Acropolis, 'Satan's Seat', as John called it, with modern Bergama sprawled untidily on the valley floor below, I became aware that I am not so haunted by her memory here as I was in Israel. The reason, as a moment's thought informed me, is that it is seven years since we took Alison round the old Province of Asia. In Israel, where we have been together so often, even during the months of her ordeal, she was a more insistent presence, a film between me and everything I looked at – the waves of her soft, silver hair, and the brown eyes which have not (alas, 'had not') changed since I knew them when she was a girl at school.

But is this what will happen, given seven years of

aloneness? I know that the loved body is gone, and that she was not, is not, it. But the shape and fashion in the brain, the mind or what you will, is all I have to hold to. I do not want it to fade, for I have said, that if there is a price to pay in the coin of pain, then I will pay it. It is a debt I owe, though she would disavow it.

'She would not wish you to suffer thus,' they tell me, meaning well. I know, I know, but would she want me to forget? A life is a whole, a tract of the only reality we know, and memory makes it so. I want the whole web of it to be perfect, and how can that be if I pluck out a part of the pattern, because the loom in its movement to and fro has begun to interweave darker threads, which, to my blurred vision, present at the moment no conformity, and appear, indeed, to spoil the past design?

Darkness has, perhaps, its place. Ferns grow under my heavier trees, those trees whose Ent-like moaning mourned her going from me. 'Supposing him to be the gardener,' perhaps ferns have a place, as she thought when she combed the bush in the ranges for them one autumn, and massed them thick in the shade west of my library windows.

April 17

DOES this record weary? Is Job wearisome? No one need read, nor need I write save that some compulsion moves me, and occasionally I seem to have some revelation of truth almost within reach. And if I write, it can only be the truth, though I desperately want, before I pause, to see some light upon the void and formless waters.

Tonight, as the sun levelled along the Maeander and Lycus Valleys, I went to the edge of the silica-coated cliff, where the lukewarm water flows to give the Laodicean epistle its imagery. It is the old site of Hierapolis. I looked south-east to Denizli, the site of Laodicea itself. The snowfields of Hormuz Dag still held the blush of sunset. The cloud-wisps over the ranges towards Ephesus, were bent and brushed to follow and reproduce the ridge tops. The valley floor, tessellated with crops, was smeared with evening mist which almost hid the river.

I felt at peace, or almost at peace, sitting there

alone, and even dared to think how we sat there with dear Alison, seven years ago. One of our people saw me sitting alone, and brought a kindly cup of coffee, at which the thin film which covers my wealthy fount of tears was broken. My mood of near peace was gone, and, incongruously, because of a lovely act of kindness.

Will it be always thus? It is strange not to be able to foretell reactions. I have always known until now that which might daunt, distress or dismay me. I deliberately avoid such areas of stress, on screen or in print. Now my reactions surprise me, and I feel I contain deep forces beyond my control. Why so changed?

April 19

I WAS right in what I said at Pergamum. We have walked through the enormous ruins of Ephesus, and twice before we have passed that way together. The footsteps on the marbled road resumed their sound beside me. I was glad.

But I was sorry I recited Callimachus' ode in the small theatre:

*They told me, Heraclitus, they told me you were
    dead,*
*They brought me bitter news to hear and bitter
    tears to shed.*
I wept when I remembered, how often you and I
*Had tired the sun with talking and sent him down
    the sky . . .*

At which the picture, half a century old, snapped into focus cruelly. Our first home, looking west, from another hill-slope, towards the ranges where we later lived . . . We would sit with our tea on trays by the front window and watch the westering sun, the red skies, 'and after that the dark . . .' And then the last lines:

*But still your pleasant voices, your nightingales
    awake*
*For Death he taketh all away but them he cannot
    take.*

I think that is how Cory rendered it, but the Greek lines in which I recited it are pure music, enough in themselves to pluck hard at the heart-strings. I got through with a choke in my voice, and even translated it, but the sheer stress gave me a few minutes of headache.

KATHLEEN

April 20

AND now Athens, with the Parthenon yonder as quietly beautiful as ever. There was no mail for me. I wish they had a post to Aslan's Country. Do they care over there? If love is care, they must, and 'God so loved the world . . .' And yet, if they care, bliss must be by that amount diminished. But need the blessed be without care, like the Epicurean gods, inanely smiling? I cannot reason it out.

E. M. BLAIKLOCK

April 25

IT is Wednesday, sixty-three weeks since the
moment in the white room when I knew that
she was gone, a safety pin, dear God, holding the
white shroud . . .

These days in Greece, where I played Gallio in
Corinth, Paul on the Areopagus, as I did the subtle
town clerk in the theatre of Ephesus, have been
packed full of talk and action. This is my land. It is
like coming home. I have spoken of all that invades
the mind. But nothing takes her presence away –
her blue hat as she sat under the 'bema' in Corinth, or by a column in the Delphi temple. But
perhaps the past has not quite so intricately interwoven the present. I learned last year that fierce
activity does for a little block the paths into the
mind, and I think I must keep unceasingly active. I
have my party interested, even entertained. The
façade is holding and I am serving others.

My bag is packed, and I write on the balcony

outside my room above the awesome Pleistos Gorge. This is goodbye to Greece. I shall not, I think, return again. Lewis brought Joy here, when they thought her cancer was gone. I brought Kath here, when we thought she had had only a slight stroke. I hoped as Lewis did. In an equal time both Joy and Kath were gone. He wrote as he wrote. I write as I write. Some of what he wrote, as I said, eludes me. Perhaps he would have words to say of my frank story – some call, perhaps, into a brighter light? Some stronger effort of faith? I can only say that all my being calls for both. Perhaps were I a better man I might be helped more strongly towards both. Perhaps God is seeking to make me a better man.

But I must school myself to live without those paroxysms of grief which filled last year. She would not like it. I shall try to cook, and discipline the mundane shape of life. But what I need and long for is some strong touch of God's hand, some absorbing new direction in life. 'Seeking a sign'? Maybe. John had only the old affirmations reaffirmed, as I did under the magnolia. It sometimes chills me, and I know that is only one of those weak and questioning words into which my frailty betrays me.

But the bus awaits to take us down to Athens, and then on to Rome. I shall take the microphone and tell of Apollo's oracle, Oedipus at the crossroads,

Helicon – as if I were unbereaved, and in my old lecture room . . . Eheu!

April 29

'SURPRISED by joy . . .' Wordsworth began in that sad poem, but agony can, in like fashion, leap out unawares, and demonstrate the fragility of the integument which covers the wound . . . In '72, she, Alison and I went into the Vatican. Alison saw the Pietá, and ran to it wondering. We joined her and saw her young face rapt and alive before that miracle of living marble.

With Anne I went up to it again. My younger granddaughter looked with the same awe. Then suddenly a slash of pain as I saw the hand of Christ. So hung her hand in the white room, when it fell back, as Alison removed her little watch, to keep, as I bade her, as a memento of our fellowship in grief. She had escaped Time, and no longer needed to measure it. Reverently, Alison slipped the silver band over her limp fingers. Pointing loosely down upon the sheet they looked like Christ's . . .

Anne looked at me, sensing something had surprised me unawares. I said nothing . . . It is curious that one of our party told me how she heard her husband fall two years ago, rushed in and found him dead. She took the watch from his limp wrist, and has worn it ever since. Another of us left us in the Corso to repeat a walk she once had with her husband. I knew him, a form ahead of me at school. Time, you see, does not heal. The task is one of courage, faith, will to conquer. It is like the task of the disabled, the halt, the lame, the blind. There is no healing, only victory to pursue, and the twisting of disaster into something God can use for others. For no other reason do I thus expose my sorrow. And meaning, I trust, will emerge from the quest. Quest? Yes, some grail to seek and courage must ride beside.

E. M. BLAIKLOCK

May 3

I AM awake early and sit with a pot of tea the night porter has brought me. We always began the day thus on the dozen occasions we have visited Stratford for a Shakespeare play ... It was 'The Merry Wives of Windsor', last night, not Shakespeare's best, but produced with gusto. At one point I laughed aloud, the first real burst of mirth since the twilight fell. Yes, I laughed, and then my eye caught the seat in front and to the right where we sat together for 'A Midsummer Night's Dream', two years ago. My laugh broke into a sob. I am not deliberately tormenting myself. It is just what happens, and she would tell me to laugh, if she could.

The *Daily Telegraph* had a paragraph this morning. At Maudling's funeral, it was at Saint Margaret's, Westminster, a Christian threnody was quoted. The words were written by Henry Scott Holland, Professor of Divinity at Oxford, a century ago: 'Death is nothing at all. I have only slipped away into the next room. Call me by my old familiar name in the easy way we always used. Put no difference in your tone, wear no forced air of solemnity or sorrow. Laugh as we always laughed at the little jokes together, play, smile, think of me.'

So she would say, and, Kath, I do thus speak to you. You would want me to laugh at Falstaff, wouldn't you? And yet, that seat hard against the stage, where she laughed at the small fairies jumping down in front of her . . . that seat.

May 10

UNTIL today, I have doubted more and more whether this small notebook should be shared with others. But I went to Dunton Green today, where the late spring was turning the Kent where she was born into tardy green.

I showed Edward England the little leather book, and he told me to finish it with what affirmations I could make. He thought it might be a help to those who find no immediate assuagement of their sorrow, those who find the common words of well-meaning comforters a little hollow, for the dried of heart, maybe, the tormented of mind. It might be good for those who look at their seniors and leaders in the Church, or in society, and think of them as being apart, invulnerable, serenely brave, and armoured against the slings and arrows which rain upon the rest.

As poor Nicias said to a doomed Athenian army outside Syracuse in B.C.: 'There is alleviation in the fact that you share it with others.' That, I have always thought, is something less than the truth, but I think it is well that all should know that testing and temptation is common to man, and I have myself always been careful not to speak with too loud and confident a voice, about that which I have not experienced. And if my cries of pain help another, I can better bear my pain, and disregard those who perhaps may sneer.

KATHLEEN

May 12

MY friends who prompted these confessions had, I am sure, too great a confidence in my fortitude of spirit, and had in mind that I might prove a torchbearer along the path to peace. A smoking brand it is that I have carried, but I have not dashed it down, nor shall I.

Have I, over the weeks of this record, made any spiritual advance? I feel sure that, after the strenuous and time-absorbing activities of leadership and lecturing which have filled these forty days, I have found an edge taken from the sharper blade of sorrow. Or is the edge of that rapier but scabbarded a little in fatigue, prompt still to rasp from its sheath and wound as it did in San Pietro and at Stratford? Time will tell, but I bid my sad fellow sufferers to cram time full, and not to sit and stare. Perhaps activity can block and choke some ploughed channels in the brain.

And, frankly, let them realise that life cannot be

E. M. BLAIKLOCK

the same again. All happiness, if happiness comes, will be muted. In spite of the old song they will never again 'come to the end of a perfect day', unless they can valiantly embrace a pattern sharpened by the darker threads. That, too, the years may bring. For brief seconds, as through a racing mist, I have thought that a little more sweetness and a little less anguish, has invaded memory as I walked today.

Happiness will never be hilarity again (and is hilarity important?). Laughter can come only as part of the public image, which it is a duty to maintain without insincerity. I grant that I cannot speak for all. A younger man might, with careful wisdom, seek to begin again and rebuild the familiar framework of life. All I say must take into account the fact that, young and active though I feel, I have lived my three score years and ten and use what they call 'borrowed time'.

For my part, I have had my message twice, coming with that simplicity which is God's way. It was given me under the magnolia tree. It was on Kath's slip of paper – 'live for others'. Perhaps, like John the Baptist, I was too expectant of a blaze from heaven. The Blue Bird, in Maeterlinck's strange play, was found, after they had searched the world, in a cage by the door. Sir Launfal, in Lowell's poem, found that the Holy Grail was the cup he had used for the beggar-man.

That, at any rate, is my determination, sharpened at this journey's end. There is a closing chapter to write in the book –

The book that God will take, my friend,
As each goes out at journey's end.

I must re-establish life's discipline, banish thoughts of death. It is possible that I must budget for a span of years, for three of my grandparents touched the middle nineties. My remaining years, how many or how few they may prove to be, must not be given to the locust. Mundane advice, and no exciting resolution, but no mystical or exalted revelations, have come my way, no Blue Bird in a magic forest, no Golden Bough.

May 13

THERE, then, is one decision made, and it will not erase the habits of a lifetime. I spoke today to a large congregation in the ancient Church of St.

Helen, Bishopsgate. Standing in the old carved pulpit during the hymn which preceded my address, I felt a twinge of pain as I looked, as my habit was, for that slightly anxious face which always watched me.

Could she possibly know? I almost felt her presence as I came to Charing Cross from Sevenoaks on the train we have so often ridden together. I must not permit myself such preoccupations. Another life, we are warned, is beyond imagining. The battle I have chosen to fight will be a lonely one. When I open the door on Friday, I shall see her chair by the window empty, as it was on April 2.

May 14

MANITOBA is below, patched with snow and frozen lakes. I have thought much on this long flight to Los Angeles, prayed wordless prayers, and asked for strength. I had hoped for serenity and for blessed fellowship in older years, but find myself with poor Robert Browning in like case:

KATHLEEN

I was ever a fighter, so — one fight more . . .
　　　　The best and the last!
I would hate that death bandaged my eyes, and
　　　　forebore,
　　　　And bade me creep past.
For sudden the worst turns the best to the brave,
　　　　The black minute's at end,
And the elements' rage, the fiend-voices that rave,
　　　　Shall dwindle, shall blend,
Shall change, shall become first a peace out of pain,
　　　　Then a light, then thy breast
O thou soul of my soul! I shall clasp thee again,
　　　　And with God be the rest!

May 18

THE lights of Auckland, says the captain, are in
view from the flight deck. There the battle
begins. But has not all my life been a battle? We
stood before the magnificent statue of Alfred
in Winchester, ten days ago, and I thought of

Chesterton's poem. The bestial Danes beat around his land.

> *And Alfred up against them bare*
> *And gripped the ground and grasped the air* . . .
>
> . . . .
>
> *With foemen leaning on his shield*
> *And roaring on him when he reeled* . . .

So often has life seemed like that, but a joyous fight it was when we held the bridge together. And yonder where the lights are a smear on the horizon, I shall stand now alone. So be it. And may the serenity I felt as I lay awake in front of the roaring turbines, continue to be mine.

For all the lesson of Sir Launfal's common cup, of the Blue Bird at the door, I thought in the night that God could have, when he has tested me, some unexpected Revelation. I am on a quest for it, as the armoured men once sought a gleaming Grail. (Why is my mind so obsessed by poetry tonight? Perhaps because she, too, loved it?)

It will happen at last, at dusk, as my horse limps
> *down the fell,*
A star will glow like a note God strikes on a silver
> *bell,*
And the bright white birds of God will carry my
> *soul to Christ,*

KATHLEEN

*And the sight of the Rose, the Rose, will pay for the
      years of hell.*

Perhaps she will come to me at that hour and we
shall journey again together. I dare not ask that the
epilogue be short, only that he give me strength to
write it well, only that he may give me 'the oil of
joy for mourning', the Spirit moving, with the gifts
of light on the darkness of the formless waters.

Wait for the Lord,
    be strong and take heart
    and wait for the Lord.

                    Psalm 27. 14. NIV

Bow down then under God's strong hand, that in his own good time he may lift you, casting all your care upon him, because he does care for you.

                    1 Peter 5. 6, 7. EMB